FACE VALUE

Is Who You See Really Who You Get?

LEGENA S. CRAWFORD

Tymm Publishing LLC
Columbia, SC

Paperback ISBN: 978-1-7330887-0-1
Ebook ISBN: 978-1-7330887-1-8

Tymm Publishing LLC
701 Gervais St, Suite 150-185
Columbia, SC 29201

Editor: Tambria Mitchell Peeples
Cover Design: Tywebbin Creations

Face Value: Is What You See What You Get?

Dedication

To my husband, Robert, thank you for your love and always pushing me to be my best self.

To my son, Logen, thank you for trying to help mommy type.

This book is also dedicated to the memory of my father the late Rev. Oliver Saxby, Jr. who inspired me to be the best and to enjoy the God kind of life.

To my mother, Elease Saxby, thank you for your unconditional love, push and support.

To Pastor Jeffrey L. Toson for your constant love, support and opportunity to minister the Gospel of Jesus Christ.

To all of my friends and family for pushing me beyond my limits.

Face Value: Is What You See What You Get?

Table of Contents

Chapter 1

It's A Beautiful Morning

"Praise the Lord everybody...Praise the Lord!" The Lord is truly in this place today. Little did I know.... there was more than the Lord in that place. Wait, what is this place?

When I woke up, I looked around and said in a whisper "Oh, my God!" now I knew calling on the name of God was breaking a commandment especially if you didn't want anything, but this time I REALLY needed Him! The night before seemed to be a blur, but I do remember that it was one that I hadn't ever experienced before or if I had, it had been a long time.

I couldn't resist his arms, his openness, his honesty, his smell, his cologne, his strength and his knowledge of all things spiritual and biblical. There was just something refreshing about his presence and what it did for me when I was around him. I mean even when he spoke, his voice sent vibrations through my body that I had not felt in a long time.

As I sat next to him, I knew the moment I longed for had to come to an end and it was back to reality. My dilemma.... how was I supposed to explain why I had been out all night? How do I explain that I was out 'counseling' and fell asleep on the couch next to a man who finally understood me? That sounds believable.... right? Then I thought maybe I didn't have to because D.J. worked last night and he would just assume that I'd fallen asleep and didn't hear the phone ring.

What was my dilemma? Well, it was almost 7a.m. and my husband normally arrives home around 7:30a.m. I knew that I wouldn't be home in time enough to even stage my being there all night.

As I continued to think about and even pray (that's some nerve huh) about how to get out of this one, I couldn't help but sink back into the arms of a man that made me forget about my worries and for a second even forget about my ten-year marriage. As I came to myself again, I began to make a move and as much as I hated to, I began to relinquish myself from the warm embrace of his arms.

"Good morning beautiful." Oh, God, not again. Do you know how long it's been since I'd heard those words?! I wanted to just melt back into his strong arms and take up residence there. *"Hey there,"* He said, with a smile like Christmas morning. *"Where are you going? I*

2

thought we'd spend the day together." Are you serious?! He wanted to spend the day.... together! I only thought, Lord, give me strength. He wanted me, he genuinely wanted me! I couldn't have asked for anything more. Well, maybe one thing more.

Although it was the moment I'd been longing for and the fulfillment of my heart's desire, there was one major roadblock...well, two major roadblocks. The one thing that would have made the moment more special was if those words had been coming from my husband. Now it wasn't that I didn't love my husband but it seems as though we had begun to grow apart. I was at a new level and it seemed as if nobody understood my growth in God but one other person and his name is Lofton... Roderick Lofton. Oh, the other roadblock? Well, I'm a pastor.

Face Value: Is What You See What You Get?

Chapter 2

How Did I Get Here?

How did I even get here? All I remember is one evening my mind was stuck on relaxing and nothing else. While at home alone on yet another evening and after being told he was off, there I was again with plenty to do but simply refused to do anything. Why? Because I was tired and just plain old fashion 'tied 'as the old folk would say. To add insult to injury, I was frustrated!

Of course, from the outside it looked as if or seemed as though everything was picture perfect. The marriage that was the envy of most appeared to be airtight. The marriage that no one expected to last was now in its 10th year run and performing week after week for "sold out" audiences in front congregations and family members alike. In my eyes, the performances were getting old and it was starting to feel like a one woman show.

Oh, see how my mind wanders, okay back to how this thing got started.

Where was I?

There I was at home alone again and although I wasn't an avid fan for so many reasons, I decided to browse around on one of the most popular social networks known to man which I dare not mention but I think everybody knows or at least has a clue.

Anyway, there I was feeling tired and frustrated and a little 'froggy' so I decided to go against the grain of my own principles. Yep, I decided to share a post. In my feeling of loneliness came forth the words... *"What do you do when weariness and frustration are your new best friends and company keepers? Is this what love does to you?"* I decided to stop there for I'd hear about it from him as this was the start of most of our moments of "intense fellowship" (thanks K.P.).

The spirit started tugging at me so I obeyed and got off because I knew something was brewing. Obedience is truly better than sacrifice and I was not in the mood for an argument. No sooner than I logged off than I got notice of a 'comment'. My first thought, "here we go...round 1!" To my surprise, it was from a visitor to my page. Oh, did I mention my page was anonymous. Well, the only person that knew it was me was my husband. The comment read "God is love and because you are made in His *image, there is no room for weariness and frustration because He longs to fill your emptiness, temper your weariness and fill your frustrations."* Ok, so

6

at this point I'm thinking who in the world is this and why has Shakespeare invaded my page...I thought he was dead! But that's not all that was said. For the second part is better than the first. "Never allow the enemy to invade your space or give him room to be your interior decorator."

"What?!" I know this can't be D.J. not that he can't write or copy from a book or something, but this is not usually how our conversations run especially from my post. Then name attached read RodLoft. Who? As you would have it, I did not hesitate to check out the profile information and to my surprise, there was no picture or pictures at all, only artwork.

Now his information indicated that he was a single man and a nonprofit organization founder. I didn't even know him or even how he got access to my page. So of course, I responded but only after I took about an hour trying to figure out who this guy was, and why he was talking to a total stranger. Then I began asking myself, "Hey, should I be talking to a total stranger?"

I was going from one level of confusion and emotion to the next (that's a whole other issue and topic altogether). But needless to say, I got up the nerve and courage to respond to Mr. Rod Loft and to my amazement it wasn't as hard as I initially thought it would be. Oh, I guess you're waiting on my reply huh? I thought long and hard about what to say and this is what I came up with... *"Thank you, but who are you?"* I know... profound, right? Well, what was I supposed to say? I mean I didn't even know this man? I waited for his reply and waited....and waited.

Now I was curious, and yeah I know what some of you are already thinking and you're probably right. If there was not response then that was my sign to stop right there not go any further so...let it go. Well, I didn't. Yes, a sister had to start praying about that thing real fast. I can imagine that a few of you are praying for me right now as you read.

A few days went by and "the comment" as I referred to it, still had yet to escape my mind. I caught myself logging on just to check to see if there were any new notifications and there wasn't even 1! Okay, my mind began to race and there was even flutter in my heart (now where that came from, I have no idea). I didn't think it was that serious. I continued to check and my excitement was completely and immediately replaced with disappointment and a tinge of anger. He has yet to respond! My thoughts not went from "what?" to "whatever!" Why did I even waste my time responding to this man? At any rate, life is about to go on.

I finally made the decision that my life would go on but little did I know things were soon about to change forever.

Legena S. Crawford

Face Value: Is What You See What You Get?

Chapter 3

Now What?

Although a few months had passed, I remember the day exactly as if it were yesterday. I was sitting at my desk on a conference call and the light on my cell began to blink. I know what you're thinking... oh ye of little faith in me. You are thinking that I immediately stopped what I was doing and grabbed my cell to check to see if it was *him*. Well, you are wrong! I at least waited until my conference call was over. I admit that I was a little anxious although I hadn't purposely thought about 'the comment' in weeks.

After my call ended, I took a deep breath and checked my inbox and to my astonishment the name that appeared was... Rod Loft. My heart said "don't," but my flesh said "why not, who will it hurt?" So, with much hesitation, I followed my head hoping that my heart would catch up. Yeah, I know what you are waiting on and thinking ...who cares about your roller coaster ride, just tell us what he said! Ok, here goes... *"Hi there, sorry it took so long for me to get back to you, but I've been out of town on business. You don't know me but I've been watching your posts for some time now as you seem to be a very talented writer. I'm actually a friend of Diahmion's. I'm sorry if I startled you but your last post concerned me and I was led to respond. Oh, please excuse my rudeness, I forgot to introduce myself, I'm Roderick Lofton."*

Did you hear that?! He said he was led to respond. Okay, okay, okay, okay, calm down. All I could respond with was, "Yeah Diahmion is a good friend and it's nice to meet you and thank you for the compliment and giving me something to think about...take care." He really didn't know how much he did give me to think about. Okay, now was the time if any to recall all of the things I'd taught and learned in all of those conferences about letting the Lord lead you and not giving in to your flesh and lustful desires. But what category did this fall in?

After reading the message, I immediately called Diahmion. As the phone rang, I was even wondering if I should let her in on the whole thing as to not make more out of it than it really was. Well, I really needed to know more about this guy so here goes. She answers, *"Hey there lady ... what's up?"*

Hey D...what's up with you girl?

"Nothing, just sitting here going over some reports...but I need a break anyway so I'm glad you called. "

"Cool, have you eaten lunch yet?"

"Nope, just about to why...what's up?"
"Hey, can you meet me at the Red Glow in about a half-hour? "

"Sure, I can be there...leaving now."

"Okay, see you in a few."

How was I supposed to get this and him off of my mind? I'm almost sure DJ would notice a difference in me. Okay, so here is the conversation I had with myself.

Okay, Lord, I know things haven't been the best between DJ and me but I really do want this marriage to work. So, what is up with this man coming from out of practically nowhere? What is up with this flutter in my heart like a schoolgirl? I love my husband... so what is this?!

Ok, so what was supposed to be an hour lunch actually turned into a dinner conversation.

Even after leaving a much-needed time with my best friend, the only thing I could think of as I drove away was what to do next.

By the time I looked up, I was at home and proceeded to pull into the garage still talking to myself with feeling God right there. I finally got out of the car and went inside but with my mind clearly on the matter at hand. When I walked through the door, there he was, the man that was given to me over 10 years ago. Here was the man who I was or am supposed to share my most intimate thoughts; the man with whom I shared my bed. Sitting there in his recliner watching basketball was the man who encouraged me (in his own way) to keep going no matter what. Don't get me wrong, my husband is still very attractive. Unfortunately, I don't know if the feeling is mutual. So if all of that is true, and it was, why was I not happy to see him? As I walked through the door, he greeted me and I got cold feet! Should I tell him how I'm feeling? If I don't, nothing will ever change or will it? I can't believe I'm saying or thinking this. Yes, me...the one who makes a living talking to Christians about their problems or concerns. What am I doing?! Ok, ok, ok (sighing) let me get myself together. As I'm off in another place, I hear, *"Hey, babe!"* as *he grabs me and kisses me on the neck. "How was your day?"*

"Hey you, it was good and how was yours?" (Did I really want to know or was I just being cordial?).

He responds, *"It was good, tired though."* Of course, to myself I thought what else is new. You're ALWAYS tired!

This is the very reason my mind began to wander in the first place. It has now been 10 years of "I'm tired" and honestly.... **"I'M TIRED!"** Tired of what seems like spinning my wheels fast and going nowhere especially in this marriage. I'm surprised he hasn't noticed yet, but hey, I guess a lot of things go unnoticed when you are too tired to pay attention. A lot like the fact that we have not been intimate in

14

almost two months. Uh, huh.... close your mouth and yes, you read right... two months and counting. Now you know why a sister can shout so long on Sunday morning, Sunday evening and Wednesday nights.

So, you see a part of me feels like I deserve a season of something fresh and new. In my mind, I believe Mr. Lofton was it. Am I thinking or talking about leaving D.J.? Of course not, well, the thought had crossed my mind once or twice but no way would I leave. Sometimes I think it would be more so to avoid all the drama it would cause and all of the questions it would raise. Besides, I really do love him.

"Chanda! I said what do you want to do about dinner?"

"Oh, uh, whatever you decide is fine with me (slight smile).

"You okay?" Yeah, I'm fine. What?! You mean he actually noticed that something was wrong? Ok... now I'm really confused... help!!!!!!!!!!!!!!

Face Value: Is What You See What You Get?

Chapter 4

I'm DONE!

I decided to go upstairs and get dressed as we decided to go out for dinner. In my mind or maybe it was hopeful thinking that this would take my mind off of the fact of the possibility of someone else occupying my mind and maybe even soon my space.

As we got in the car, I tried to share conversation with him about how glad I was to be with him and how I so needed the outing and hopes of having dessert that was not on the menu. I reached my hand over to massage his neck as a gesture of my hopes of making that last statement true and to no avail, did he respond with a *"Dang, not so hard"*. As the air deflated out the balloon that I was starting to fill with the air of promise and hope, I simply removed my hand and sat quietly. There shortly after, we pulled up to the restaurant and surprisingly, he come around and opened my door. Needless to say, my mind had already started to wander. Would Lofton have enjoyed the massage and how would he walk around and open my door? I got out of the car with a smile on my face as I had drifted off and when I heard the voice, there was a snap of reality that brought me back. I'm glad my thoughts were still held captive by my tongue and my mouth as to not have escaped yet. *"Oh, thank you,"* I responded after getting out of the car.

"Where were you just now?" he said.

"Huh?"

"You looked like you were in another world just now... where were you?"

Oh wow! Lord, please help me to stay focused! This thing is getting dangerous.

We made it through dinner and went home and had "dessert". I had a taste of EVERYTHING that was on the menu that he had to offer. I must say that I was quite surprised that it was even there to offer to me. So, I know beyond a shadow of a doubt that this is it for my daydreaming, thought stealing, mind wandering antics regarding Mr. Lofton. Whew... glad that's over... or so I thought.

The next morning there was deep meditation and the prayer and hope that things had finally begun to shift in our favor. I arose out of the bed in hopes to share a blissfully wonderful morning conversation and lo and behold to my surprise yet again... there was none. What?! You mean after a wonderful night like last night, it's back to the way it was just that fast?! Are you serious?!!!!!!!! Ok, I can

Legena S. Crawford

do this. Don't get annoyed but just go and have a little talk with Jesus and everything will be alright. I thought for sure that we made some progress.

The way I'm feeling now, somebody needs to know that I am NOT happy. This is the final straw... social media I hope you are ready for this!

As I posture myself, my post reads...

"Soooo what do you do when love takes place under false pretense? The words you once spoke and the way you once made me feel are now a distant memory. I'm DONE!"

As much as I hate it when other people blast their business out there for all of society to see, here I was giving into temptation yet again. I let the world know how unhappy I am with this man who keeps playing these games with me and calling it love!

Yeah, I did it again and don't think I really cared who saw it. Well, in the back of my mind, I was hoping that one person in particular would see it. Maybe he wouldn't respond and I can get so angry that he will conveniently just go away. Well, I waited and waited and waited. It had been three weeks now and still no response from him. Good... I was finally in the clear or so I thought.

19

Face Value: Is What You See What You Get?

Chapter 5

Flight, Fight or
Just Plain Fright?

I was up late one night and writing a bible study lesson and from time to time peeking over at DJ as he slept so soundly and to my astonishment, there was a light blinking on my phone. I actually thought that I had turned it off before I began to study. I grabbed my phone and started to turn it off when my curiosity got the best of me and against my better judgment, I decided to check to see who it was. Well I mean just in case there was someone, a member, trying to get in contact with me (yeah, I had to convince myself that was the truth too).

When I pressed the button, it again was a moment that I would change my life forever. I checked the message and there it was again, the man that would change my life forever. It was Mr. Lofton. What?! Why now?! Why again?! Ok, so there must be something going on that I just don't quite seem to understand. I thought that this thing was over. I mean it had been three weeks! Then the thoughts began to infiltrate my mind again. Should I even bother to answer or should I just delete the number altogether? But if I delete the number, I would never know what this thing is about or what I'm supposed to get from this. So, I decided to read the message. *"Hi, I hope all is well with you. I saw your post and was hoping that you didn't forget our first conversation regarding your space... RodLoft."*

Forget! Are you kidding? How could I forget the words that made me regenerate the way I think about this thing called life and the way I have been letting it live me and not me live it. Okay, seriously, it was time for me to really sit down and take the time to figure out what the heck was really going on. I mean, me, the Pastor, the Counselor, the wife, the one that EVERYONE comes to in THEIR time of need for advice. So.... what I am to do now? Who am I supposed to go to and tell that I am having thoughts about another man and I might actually enjoy whatever this is supposed to be. I mean I do run the risk of exposing so much of myself and we ALL know with the latest headlines about 'God's elect', that is **NOT** one battle I am willing to fight.... or am I?

I mean it's to the point where my mind is beginning to wonder if this is the thing is supposed to propel me into the me I'm supposed to be, the me I am longing to be. Was this my way of escape?

AHHHHHHH!!!!!!!

Okay, bring it back and breathe in deep sistah. I mean the Word does say that "ALL things work together for the good of them that love the Lord and are called according to His purpose." I never thought that I would see the day that I would even question my calling and purpose. Is there really a purpose for whatever this thing is? Now the bigger question is whether I should respond to him or not. Not hearing from him is such a long time has allowed me to have a way of escape. However, the problem is I have not escaped it in my mind. I realized that I had to be completely honest with myself and already knowing that I wanted to respond just to see where this is taking me. I think I'll sleep on it.

Face Value: Is What You See What You Get?

Chapter 6

This Thing

As I nestled in during the evenings, I was not tired physically, but tired from thinking all day about what to do. I noticed I started getting home kinda late (on purpose) just so I wouldn't have to face DJ whose shift had now changed, and I thankfully he would already be half asleep. As to not wake him up, I just kinda settled in down stairs in my office because I really needed some time alone. I often felt a small sense of regret that I had not been there lately. I mean this thing is truly starting to consume me. I had always promised myself that this would never happen to me. I mean really, how many times have I counseled others on how to avoid these kinds of things and how I prided myself in having the 'perfect' marriage and the almost 'perfect' life. God sure does have a sense of humor. Where was this man 10 years ago when I was ready for this?

The first thing I should have done was to pray and ask God for guidance. I can tell you I think I was beginning to regret what I started. Apparently, I wasn't regretting it enough because I still pondered to how to respond to Mr. Lofton. After a long debate with myself, I decided to inbox him. Yeah, I know what you're thinking and believe me, I knew there would be consequences but I didn't care. I just cared that there was finally somebody who cared about what I thought and somebody who finally would listen to me and understand my deeper thoughts. I didn't care that it was not the man God had led to me. Maybe it was because I knew forgiveness would come later and I was willing to pay the price now.

Before I logged on, I made sure the house was quiet and that I was in a position to hear if my DJ decided to wake up in the middle of the night and question what I was doing. I already had my excuse concocted that I was working on a special project. Well, I wouldn't be telling a lie. I was actually working on a project. Ok, so the project I was working on was my life but a project nonetheless. I was trying to figure out what I had gotten myself into and curious as to how this "thing" was going to work out. Well, here I go.

The whole while I was logging on, I kept thinking about what I was about to do. Yes, I did think about it and for some reason, I felt like I deserved it. I began to think about all of the years of sacrifice I'd given to this marriage, to the ministry and in this life. No sooner had I logged on than a message popped up from... yes, Mr. Lofton. I hesitated and just decided what the heck. I saw him on the chat line and decided to chime in without even reading his message. "Hi" was all I could muster up enough to get out. Yeah, pitiful I know.

I sat and waited, although embarrassed. It had been about 20 minutes and I started to feel like a fool and just as I was about to log off, the words *"I've been waiting and wondering"* popped up. Needless to say, my heart, once again, began to palpitate and I was once again reeled in just after I'd decided to save myself the unnecessary drama. I mean I really did not get it. Every time I was about to let this thing go, it decided to stay. The question still remained...why?

"Waiting and wondering?"

"Yes, I thought you had decided it was too much for you to think about and you decided to let it go."

It was like this man was inside of my head... I mean...what the heck?! I had to get me a drink! Not what you think.... a simple glass of water (ice cold water with extra ice).

"No. I too was waiting and wondering where you had gone. Too much...you care to elaborate?"

"I didn't know if what I had said to you was out of the way or seemed to boisterous seeing as to how we've never formally met."

"No, it's nothing that I can't handle. I have actually been thinking about what you've said to me over the past few weeks and how did you even come up with that. I mean, you don't even know me."

"I know you more than you think I do. There is just something about you and the words you choose to press upon the pages when you do decide to press."

"So... how long have you been 'impressed' with me, I mean my words?"

"Ha, ha, ha, ha. See I told you that there was something about you. It's been a while. I was not comfortable sharing with you although I wanted to for quite some time. Once I found out that you and I are mutual friends with Diahmion then I felt it was okay to proceed. Let me assure you that I am not up to anything, but really just enjoy your writing. It's been a minute since I've seen or even heard of somebody with your style and when I saw the most recent post, I just got concerned and had to reach out to you. I really hope you don't mind."

Uhhhhh...did he say mutual friends with Diahmion?! You mean to tell me she knew this man and NEVER said a word about him. Wait until I talk to her again. Ok, let me focus, let me focus.

"No. I mean, yeah. Okay let me start over. I mean no, I'm cool with you reaching out to me and yes, it's okay and well.... Just thank you for the compliments."

28

Oh, Lord. Can you believe I started to fumble like that?! Really?!!!!!!! Well, the conversation kept going and when I looked up, my eyes began to bulge because the clock said 5:00 a.m. Are you serious?! We have literally chatted all night and well into the next morning. It was almost time for the alarm clock to go off and for DJ to wake up. I decided to jump into bed and pretend like nothing had happened. Before I knew it, the clock went off and a new day had begun. Lord, talk about sleepy! Yes, I was.

Face Value: Is What You See What You Get?

Chapter 7

A Temporary Normal

I tried my best to go about the morning like normal but all I could think about was the conversation that was held only a few hours ago. I was sleepy and tired in the physical but there was something going on in my spirit that had me leaping for joy. I really didn't understand this and was more confused now than ever before! What was I supposed to do now for real? I know it was only a conversation and that this man and I had never even met face to face but I just felt a connection there.

"Babe, babe, ... BABE!"

Is that DJ calling me? "Oh, huh, I'm sorry love, what's up?"

"Uh, I was waiting on a goodbye kiss. You okay?"

Okay, honey, get it together. You are slippin' already and it's not even that kind of party that you should be forgettin' the routine set for its 10th year. Bring it back sweetie, bring it back.

31

"Oh, babe, I'm sorry, I just had a long night trying to get this project ready and all. Have a good day (smack on the lips)." I did notice he hesitated because the smack was usually a wet one that he usually despised and had to walk away wiping.

As I began to collect my thoughts, get ready and head to the church, I couldn't help but replay the conversation. On the way to the church office for the day, I decided to check my email in hopes of a message (I must admit) and there it was.... absolutely nothing! I felt like a fool even checking to see if it was him. This time, I was certain that I had made up in my mind to just let this thing go. No sooner again as I was getting in the car I heard my phone give an alert. It was usually around the time DJ sent his daily message so I didn't even bother to check it (sad I know). I kept driving almost in a daze. My alert went off again and I was sure that it was Diahmion trying to reach me.

Needless to say, it was hard to stay focused the entire day. In order to get anything done, I forced myself to ignore the alert again and again. When I finally got in the house and got settled, I decided to check my phone and to my surprise, I had three messages from Mr. Lofton. It tried to hide my excitement. All through dinner, I was waiting for DJ to turn in early. You would know it that Mr. decided he wanted to get close tonight and of course I had to oblige him. I mean we are still married.

After he had gone to sleep, I went back to work on my 'special project'. It was my hope that it was not too late to respond. Oh, I know you are curious as to what the messages said huh? Well, okay, I guess I can share.

"Hi, there. Just wanted you let you know I truly enjoyed our conversation yesterday, well today (LOL). Was wondering if you were available to read something for me as I'd really appreciate your thoughts and opinion?" Let me know if you are interested." RodLoft.

Interested?!!!! He just didn't know how interested I was (in his writing of course or so I was convincing myself). What should I say? By the way, Diahmion STILL had not made mention of him. This time I didn't even hesitate to respond. I told myself to keep it short and simple only *myself* chose **not** to listen and before I knew it, I had written at least two full paragraphs!

"Hi Rod. I hope you don't mind me calling you that. I would be delighted to read what you have and thank you for thinking enough of me to be able to share. I too was sitting here working on some things of my own and I guess if you are willing to share then I don't see why I can't do the same I mean only if you don't mind of course. I am very overprotective of my work and if you are anything like me would love to share it with someone I know who would appreciate it and the thoughts behind it.

Please feel free to send it over to me at my personal email address listed on my info and actually, you can feel free to give me a call at any time. I am usually free any time after..."

As I was about to share my availability, I heard a noise coming from the bedroom and had to hurry up and silence my swag if you will.

"Hey, what you still doing up?" asked DJ.

"Oh, hey, I couldn't sleep and just decided to get an early start on my sermon for Sunday. Why are you up... I mean are you okay?"

"Yeah, I just had to use the bathroom and noticed you weren't in bed. Maybe I'll get some work done myself since I'm not really sleepy anymore."

Ugh! What was I supposed to do now?! I really wanted to finish my thoughts to Rod. I guess this was the perfect example of divine intervention.

"Oh, no baby, I mean you have to get up early in the morning don't you and you really need to get some sleep. Sooooo, why don't you just go lay down and you will eventually fall back to sleep."

We sat in silence for a few seconds, me all the while ignoring the divine intervention piece hoping and praying that DJ would return to the bedroom. After about a minute or two, he finally decided to get up and go back into the room.

"Hey, you need to come to bed too."

"Okay honey, let me get these last few thoughts out and I'm on the way. Love you... good night."

Really? Did I really just hit a falsetto note with that bit of fluff? Well, it wasn't all fluff as I really do love my husband but....ok, anyway, back to completing my thoughts. I went on to tell Rod the specific times that he could call me and then I proceeded to go to bed as I promised but with a big smile on my face. It was a good thing that DJ didn't have eyes in the back of his head and was a heavy sleeper or else I would have had a lot of explaining to do.

I finally made it to sleep somewhere around 5 a.m. I must have been really tired because the only reason I work up was because the phone rang. I looked over at the caller ID and the number to the church appeared. Huh, why would someone be calling me from the church this early in the morning?

"Hello."

"Good afternoon, Pastor this is Brother Taylor."

"Yes, hello Brother Taylor. How are you? Is everything alright?"

"Uh, yes Pastor. We were just calling to see if everything was okay with you?"

"Oh, yes, Brother Taylor I am fine, why do you ask"?

"Well, you missed this morning's meeting with the Deacons and the community board is sitting here waiting now."

"But it's only..." I turned to look at the clock and to my surprise, it was already 1 p.m.! What happened?! How in the world did I sleep until 1pm and why didn't DJ wake me up before he left?! Okay, I had to get myself together and regroup.

"Uh, Brother Taylor, please let the board know that I am on my way as we speak and try to stall them 'til I get there. You know what to say. Lead 'em in a song or two or three." The way Brother Taylor sings, pray, and shout that should hold'em for at least 30 to 45 minutes. I got up and took a very quick pick me up bird bath and headed for the door.

No sooner had I gotten into the car that my phone rang yet again. Okay, now I know Brother Taylor couldn't be finished that fast. As I looked at my phone and was ready to ask Brother Taylor to either sing another song or take them on a tour of the church, I noticed that the area code was 123. Who is this? It just so happens that they left a voicemail. I was already late to my meeting so I didn't have time to stop and take a listen as I needed to concentrate on getting to the church.

I finally made it just as the board members were about to leave. I offered my deepest apologies and practically had to beg and bribe them to stay to have the meeting. Needless to say, I got some very interesting looks. Nevertheless, the meeting proceeded. In the midst of the meeting, I couldn't help but allow my mind to drift back to the number I saw on my phone. Was it him? As the meeting continued, I excused myself from the table and ran to the restroom as I couldn't wait any longer. I called my voicemail and yes it was him! I began to do a happy dance with a smile on my face. He said that he was sorry to disturb me and that he wanted to meet me at the coffee shop downtown. Meet....in public? Oh, now that was a different story. Ok, genius...now what? It was time I stop to really think about what I was doing. But hey, I mean this was innocent right? I hadn't committed any crime of sorts.

Face Value: Is What You See What You Get?

Chapter 8

A New Level of Wrong

I ran back to the meeting and actually focused on what we were talking about. After the meeting ended, I immediately called him and said that we could meet but suggested that we did it at a coffee shop about 45 minutes away. As I was headed that way, he agreed. I couldn't run the risk of being seen with another man and if I did, I had already made up in my mind that it would have been a counseling session.

On the drive there, I couldn't believe that I was actually going to do this. I pulled up and had no idea what I was getting myself into. I got out of the car and slowly walked in. I looked around the place and found an empty space to sit. I hadn't been there for even five minutes and I was already wanting to leave, but just when I had made up my mind that this was not a good idea, there he was. He called my name *"Chanda?"* I swear I had never heard my name called like that ever before. There he was, this tall dark chocolate man with the muscles that looked like mountains spewing forth from the dirt of God's green earth. He had a voice like thunder and teeth like diamonds! Honey, all I could do was pray! Really, Lord.... really? Why couldn't he at least be 5 foot 4, 300 pounds with a gold tooth in the front? That would have helped me make my decision so much better and easier.

"Yes, it's me...Rod?" He nodded and we shook hands. *"Please have a seat."* My heart was beating so loud that I could hardly hear myself talk. If this was *just* a meeting about his work, then why was I so nervous? Okay... get it together here.

"So, it's nice to finally meet you. Did you have a problem finding the place?"

"No, no problem finding it. I didn't even know it was here but it seems to be a pretty nice spot. You come here often?" he asked.

"I come here from time to time just to have some time to myself or to clear my head." There was an awkward silence so I tried to keep thinking of what to say. "So, how long have you been writing?"

He started to explain about his writing and all I could do was stare at him. Lord knows I was trying my best to listen. The conversation continued and we looked at his writings and I told him a little bit about mine and before I know it, I glanced at my phone and it was 8 o'clock! What was I thinking... how did I spend

4 hours talking to this man?! Ok, there was no time to panic but regroup. How was I going to explain this? Oh, I guess I forgot to mention that bible study started at 7pm! Twice in one day... ugh, what is going on? I really don't understand what's happening.

"Oh, look at the time. I'm sorry, I've gotta go... I'm late."

"Oh, Chanda, I'm sorry to keep you. Can I call you or can we meet again?"

"Huh? Yeah... sure." I hurried out the door not realizing what I just said.

I could not believe that I did this again! I was driving so fast and praying that God would show me favor as I was hoping not to get a ticket. Ok, I had to hurry up and get my mind into preacher mode. I was really afraid to even look at my phone as I know that I would have several missed calls and messages wondering where I was. No sooner had I said it, the phone rang. It was DJ. Okay, here we go with the 20 questions so let me prepare my mind.

"Uh, um.... hello."

"Hey, you alright.... you know you late right?"

"Yes, I know and I'm on my way. I just got caught up in a meeting with a friend but I'm on my way."

"Yeah, okay.... you might wanna hurry. Folks looking kinda disgruntled. Brother Taylor said this is the second time today. What's up with you? You know what, never mind. Just get here before Sister Wyatt start riot. You already know you are not her favorite person anyway."

"I'm driving as fast as I can okay...just tell them I'm coming."

I finally pull up to my parking space and wouldn't you know it, the place is packed tonight. Okay, don't get excited. Lord, you know I really need you right now to get through this next hour. Well, I mean I need you way, way after that too but for right now... I REALLY need you! I got out of the car and begin to thank God that my track skills kicked in because I had to literally run down the hall in right into the sanctuary. When I opened the door, of course all eyes turned to me. I just politely walked in and sat to the side as Co-Pastor Chamblee was about to go into the closing prayer. He turned and saw me and decided to turn the remainder of the service over to me. Ok Lord, here we go.

"Thank you, Pastor Chamblee and good evening, everyone. It is so good to see all of you in the house tonight. My apologies for missing what I know was an absolutely terrific evening with the Lord. I was caught up in a much needed counseling session trying to convince one to turn their life over and come on over to the Lord's side. I have faith and confidence that Pastor Chamblee blessed you with a mighty word." I had to wait a while for the applause to calm down. This was a good thing. At least I know they weren't too mad.

"Ok, ok that's enough, I'm still the Pastor y'all." I had to be sure to break any ice that was left unthawed just in case there were a few icebergs left sitting in place. "May the peace of God be with each of you as you leave this place until you return by His grace. Amen, Amen and Amen."

Thank you, Lord, for getting me through that even though I knew I had hit an all-time low. A much needed counseling session... really?! I had to go down and greet the congregation but in the midst of doing so, my mind drifted back to where I'd left. I hope I wasn't too rude to Rod. Okay honey, focus! After greeting the last person, I was on the way down the hall to my office when I got stopped again with the call of my name.

Chapter 9

Operation Concentration

"Pastor Childs!"

Lord can I just get to my office in peace. Oh but wait, I recognize that voice. I couldn't help but to stop with a smile on my face.

"Yes, my sister, how may I help you?"

"Uh, you can start by telling me where you been."

"I know you ain't trying to check the Pastor."

"Uh, does the Pastor wanna keep gettin' a check?"

"Hey D, what's up girl?"

"Uh, I should be asking you what's up. Where have you been? Not once but late twice today ma'am?"

"I know, I know. I don't know how time just got away from me today. I just lost track of time I guess and don't look at me like that."

"Uh, huh."

"I had a meeting with someone who needed some counseling and it ran kinda late." I hope she couldn't sense that I was getting a little nervous. At least I didn't have to lie. I mean he did ask for some advice and it did run a little late.

"Yeah, ok. You got me this time. I'll call you later girl... bye."

"Byyeeeeeee." It was so hard not to mention her knowing Rod.

That was the easy one to have to explain to. Now I had to worry about going home and explaining things to DJ. I just know he is not going to remotely understand this. I mean he's not going to understand me. Not Miss "Always gotta be on time." How in the world was I going to explain being late twice in the same day?! Ok. I'll just tell him the exact same thing that I told Diahmion and make sure I say it while looking him right in the eyes with a straight face. I was pulling up in the driveway bracing myself for what was about to happen.

"Hey, babe."

"Hey. How was your day? Busy I take it?" Here we go out the gate with the sarcasm.

"Yeah. It was"

"Aiight, I'm gone to bed. Good night." (Kisses me on the lips)

"Good night." That's it? What happened to the drill? Are you serious? I mean I had my explanation down this time and all I get is a good night? Wow! Hey. Does that mean that I'm off the hook? I should be happy.... right?

Wrong. Why was he not questioning me? Hmmmm. I am going to call this a day and get some sleep and try this again tomorrow.

Just as I was on my way upstairs and was about to turn off my cell phone, I looked and saw that I had a message. Uh, I just don't have enough energy to even listen to anybody else today.   I glanced again and didn't quite recognize the number. Okay, last one for the road. As I listened, this is what I heard...

"Hey there Chanda this is Rod. Uh, I was just checking to make sure everything was okay because you left in kind of a hurry. Okay, just give me a call when you get a chance. I would love for us to finish what we started... our conversation that is (laughs).   Well, hope to hear from you soon...good night."

Now that is just what I needed to send me off to la la land. After hearing that, all I could do is just stop a minute on the stairs and sit. I couldn't go to bed just yet because I already know what's going to happen. My mind would be stuck and I do mean stuck on Mr. Lofton. I have got to get this thing back in order.   So I decided to pray that the mood will kick in and Bro. Childs and I can have some time to shine. I decided to slip into something a little grown up and be a blessing. I decided to turn on some music which I knew would get his attention. I was already prepared and just when I thought he was looking, this is what I hear...
"zzzzzzzzzzz, pause, zzzzzzzzzzz."

What?! Are you for real? That did it, I can't take it anymore. This is really about to work my nerves. Of course now my mind went directly back to the place it had been before this little escapade. I could have done one of two things. I could have either prayed, pout, suck it up and go to bed or I could breath and make a call. I think you know which one I decided to do. Yep, off to my office I went to make the call. I was hoping that it wasn't too late. Well, here I go.

"Hello, Chanda?"

"Uh, hi. I didn't wake you did I? I was just returning your call. If it's too late, I can always call you back tomorrow or some other time."

"(Laughing) No, you're good. Why put off tomorrow what you can do today? I was just wanting to make sure everything was okay. I mean when you left today, you were kind of in a hurry."

"Oh yeah, I'm good. I just forgot another appointment that I had. But it all worked *out...thanks. That was really sweet of you* to check on me. I apologize for that. So, I really enjoyed talking to you and your work is awesome! It's very intriguing. What's your inspiration?"

"Oh, man thanks. Uh, I just write what come to my mind. You talk about me, I can say the same about you if not more. That's what drew me to you in the first place."

"Oh, I should be thanking you. I was just writing one night and really didn't think

48

anything of it. I mean, it's a passion of mine but not something I look to make public or go viral or anything."

"Why not?"

"Why not what?"

"Why not let other people read what you are saying? I mean, if I was a blessing to me to take notice, I'm sure it would be a blessing to so many others. It might even save a life."

As the conversation went on, I tried so darn hard to keep my composure. This man was talking about me and interested still in me! This is something that DJ and I NEVER talk about. He was talking about blessing people and saving people's lives with my writing. I still didn't have the courage to tell him that this is what I already do every day as a pastor. Why was this so hard to do? Was I ashamed to say it for fear that he wouldn't understand or was I tired of being who I am?

We went on again to chat for another hour or so and then I looked up and yet again it was well after 2am. I couldn't risk another day being late so I ended the conversation. He asked if I was free to meet again later that same day and I told him that I would have to check my schedule. I didn't want to make myself too available. (Laugh) Listen to me. Ugh. What was I really getting myself into? I had again tried to convince myself that it was all and really about his and my writing and how we could go to the next level. Was I really fooling myself? (Yawn) Lord, you have got to clear my mind.

I woke up the next morning in time to see DJ off to work and even fix him a nice breakfast. Yeah, he was surprised but seemed to enjoy it. I think talking to Rod actually helped me to get up and get things in gear. Was I really cooking for DJ or was I thinking about Rod in the back of my mind? That is something now that I contend with all the time lately.

It turned out to be a really good day as I made it to all of my appointments on time and stayed in a very cheerful mood for the entire day. I was willing to forgive DJ and try the husband and wife plan again tonight. He was shocked at how energetic I was but it turned out to be a VERY good evening for the Childs family (smile). It was so nice that I didn't even give Mr. Lofton a single thought or a call.

I was convinced that for just that brief moment our time together was what I needed to get the flame rekindled in my marriage. It was good for a few days and then the call came. I didn't listen to the message right away because, well I finally lost interest. Then the day came when DJ and I had a slight (in my eyes) disagreement about him being 'tired' again and I had the urge to listen to my messages.

"Chanda, this is Rod. Haven't heard from you in a while and was just calling to make sure everything was okay. Give me a call when you

get a chance. I have something new I wanna run past you."
Sigh.

Chapter 10

Decisions, Decisions

Okay Chanda. Don't do it. Don't call him back. You can work this thing out with DJ. Girl, it's okay if you call him back. I mean it's just about the projects he's working on. And you heard what he said about blessing folk and stuff.

What in the world is going on?! NO!!! I was having a conversation with myself and confused myself! I recognized the angelic voice on one shoulder and then the little 'devilena' on the other. I was not believing this! You know what, I am going to meet this thing head on and get it over with for good. I dialed the number and it went straight to voicemail. Maybe if I leave a message that would suffice.

"Hi, Rod. It's Chanda. I got your message and look, I don't think it's a good idea for us to meet again. I mean it has nothing to do with you or your writings. You just caught me in a bad place right now and..."

"Hey, hey, hello.... Chanda?"

Dang! He picked up the phone.

"Oh, hey Rod, I was just leaving you a message. Uh, I don't think we'll be able to get together anymore, you see I..."

"Oh, did I do or say something?"

"No, you just caught me in a bad or a very interesting place right now.

"I was just concerned because I hadn't heard from you in a few weeks and wanted to make sure everything was okay with you. I didn't mean to scare you or anything."

"Oh, no, you didn't scare me (laughing) I was just taking some time to spend with my husband and trying to work some things out."

"Ahhh, wow... husband. Man, Chanda, I am sooooo sorry. Look I didn't even think to ask about a husband or boyfriend. Look, if I need to explain anything, I'd be more than happy to. I would never intentionally come between you and your husband."

"No Rod, it's cool. I should have mentioned it and just didn't. We'd been going through some things and I really thought your writing and our conversations were refreshing." I think I owe you an apology for not saying anything."

"Look, I am not for breaking up homes Chanda. I just really wanted to connect with you because of the inspiration you have given me these past few weeks but if it's going to cause any issues with your husband then, hey, I agree that we shouldn't continue this."

What...he agreed?! Oh, no he didn't! The last thing he was to supposed to do is agree with me. I mean what kind of man is he?! Here I was ready with my speech as to why we couldn't continue this and he didn't even give me the chance to give it because he agreed with me. Ok, so what I am supposed to do now? Think, think, think...THINK!!

"Well, he understands that I come in contact with new people all the time and doesn't have a problem with it." He doesn't have a problem with it because he doesn't know about it. But that's beside the point.... I think. "So, I mean we can still get together because I'm looking for that person to push me and give me the boost I've been needing and lo and behold...here you are."

"So, you're sure he won't mind?"

"Oh, no... he won't mind at all." Cause I ain't never gonna tell him. But there was no need to disclose that information to Rod.

"Okay so now where were we (smiling)? I tell you what, I have some time tomorrow morning if you'd like to look over some things."

"If you're sure then tomorrow morning works for me. Let's say about 10am?"

"Sounds good to me. See you then."

"I'm looking forward to it. Have a good night."

"Thanks, you too."

Here I go again with this smile on my face. I can't lie and say that I wasn't glad to hear from him. I was.

As the evening went on, DJ decided to surprise me with dinner. It's been quite a long time since he's done anything like that and I was truly surprised. Then he hit me with the big one!

"Hey babe, what are you doing tomorrow?"

"Tomorrow? Uh...why do you ask?"

"I've been thinking and I decided to take the entire day off to spend time with you."

He decided to take the day off of work tomorrow? What?! Are you serious? Now, all this time Rod had been gone and now he decides he wants to take the day off. Ok Lord, here we go again with these decisions.

"Oh, baby that's sweet of you. The only thing I have is a meeting at 10 a.m. but that's really about it."

"Oh, you got to meet at the church because if so I can go with you and we can just take one car and leave from there."

Really? Now what am I supposed to say to that, no you can't go cause I'm meeting the man who is responsible for rekindling and refreshing something in me?

"Oh, no it's not at the church but I'll see if I can't change it for another day." Whew! I guess I bought some more time to really think about some things. *"So what do you have in mind?"* I had to act interested because if I didn't more questions were sure to come.

"Now if I told you then it wouldn't be a surprise."

The next morning, we got up and got dressed and I tried to call Rod that night before but DJ was literally all up under a sista (not that opposed it). What is wrong with me?! The first thought of the morning was not on the day DJ had planned, but on the idea that I didn't want to disappoint Rod. I went into panic mode but why? Why was I not excited about spending time with my husband? Had we gotten so far gone until my feelings have just dissipated completely? I heard a knock on the bathroom door...dang!

"Hey babe, you alright in there? You been in there for a good lil minute. We gotta go in about 15 minutes."

What...15 minutes?! What was the rush? I'm trying to get in touch with Rod to let him know I can't meet him in addition to trying to get myself together enough to spend time with my husband without him noticing my self-created drama. Now how in the world am I supposed to do all of that in 15 minutes?! Huh....answer me?! Oh Lord, am I really talking...no yellin' at myself? Ok, let me get it together.

"I'll be right out love... I'm finishing up now." I had to at least try one more time to get Rod. Ok, it's ringing... dang, it went straight to voicemail.

"Chanda, let's go!"

"Comin'! Hey Rod, it's Chanda. Um, I tried to reach you earlier to let you know that I won't be able to make it this morning...uh something came up. But I will try to give you a call or text a little later. (sigh) Bye."

Chapter 11

Savoring the Suspect

Where in the world are we going? We have been in this car for three hours already and for some reason I can't get a signal on my phone. DJ has been talking to me the entire time or at least trying to make conversation. I hope I have been giving the right answers because I really don't think I have been listening. So we finally get to where we're going and it really is a beautiful place in the mountains as we pull up to this cabin. Cabin? So that means that we are spending the night and that means that I won't be back home until tomorrow or the day after? And that now means no contact with Rod. Ok. Maybe this is God's way of getting this man out of my system once and for all.

We get in and get settled and as I am having a change of heart and mind, my expectations are once again shot to heck. All of a sudden, I hear snoring from the other room. Yes, snoring! You mean to tell me that you drove me three hours away from home to fall asleep?! Okay, don't snap Chanda, don't snap. This is the perfect time for you to do some major reflecting. So, I let him sleep because granted he has worked along week and is seemingly trying to make this work.

I decided to stay in the living room and just chill when low and behold, I hear a ding coming from my phone. Wait, I thought the reception was bad out here. I walked over to pick up my phone and realize that it's not my phone that the ding is coming from but DJ's. So, yeah before you even ask, I decided to pick it up and check to see what or who was making contact. I mean, he was asleep and it could be something important. So I pick up the phone and in big bold letters, I see these words... "SORRY I COULDN'T MAKE IT THIS WEEKEND. I TRIED TO CALL YOU TO TELL YOU MY PLANS CHANGED AND CAN MEET YOU THERE IF THE OFFER IS STILL OPEN." What in the world?! So, you mean all this time I have been trying to get rid of these whatever this is for Rod and DJ is doin' his own thing. Ok...what is this? I mean wow! This was the LAST thing I expected. Had I neglected him that much for him to find somebody else? So, what do I do now? Well, I decided not to go into panic mode and but to text back. So here goes.

"WASSUP? I'M GLAD TO HEAR FROM YOU AND SORRY YOU COULDN'T COME

WITH ME BUT I DECIDED TO BRING MY WIFE INSTEAD."

I waited and waited for the return text and tried my best not to go on a smacking spree.

Is this why I was so smitten with Mr. Lofton? Was it my instinct that caused me not to be able to forget my recent encounter? As I sat contemplating how to make my discovery known to the right Deacon, the phone made a sound. It was the return text I had been waiting for. As I proceeded to pick up the phone, I was startled by DJ entering the room. Dang! I was so close to finding out what was really going on. I was almost sure he'd know I had been tampering with his phone. Okay ......here we go with the fireworks.

What?!

Ooohhhh no! Remember those fireworks I was waiting on, well they fizzled before even gettin' off the ground. All he did was walk over to the phone pick it up, took a short glance and put it down. As a matter of fact, to make things worse, he decided to turn the sucker off! Now how am I supposed to sneak and look at it if it's turned off....is nothing sacred anymore?!

What now? That's the question that is plaguing my mind as he moseys his way over to me and proceeded to hug up on a sista as if nothing had happened. Lord, you have got to help me today. What am I supposed to do now? Am I supposed to act as though I had not seen the text and even more, was I supposed to act as though I was not still thinking about Mr. Lofton. There was no doubt about it... I was losing it and started to confuse myself.

So, I tried to put things out of my mind and allowed him well us to get our God given groove on. As I tried to think pleasant thoughts, I still contemplated bringing up the text I saw. For some reason, something was telling me that now was not the right time. DJ had drifted off to sleep and I was still wide awake as my mind continued to wander. As you very well may already know, I was thinking about my own phone and wondering if I had any messages myself. I decided to slide from underneath his grip and go outside (scared and all with the sounds of nature) and turn on my phone. Low and behold, there were a few messages. There were ten to be exact.

As I listened, most of them were about the church and just as soon as I was about to hang up assuming they were all about sister or brother so and so and about a few meeting reminders, there was the last one where I heard a voice that said he was sorry that we could not meet and how much he was looking forward to our conversation among other things. Among other things......that was new. I tried my best not to have the desire to call him back and no sooner had I began to dial the number, DJ came out to see where I was.

"Oh, hey babe. I was just checking my phone for any church messages. Why are you up? I didn't wake you, did I?"

"No babe, I went to the bathroom and you weren't there.... you okay?"

"Yeah, I'm fine. I just needed to get some fresh air that's all." I wonder if he could see right through that lie because a lie it was. Then again, maybe it wasn't because I truly did need some fresh air because little did he know I knew he was livin' foul. Somethin' on the inside of that cabin was funky and it wasn't me.

Let's just say the next two days were blissfully torturous. In other words, we made up for lost time but my thoughts were still lingering in the air like that big, humongous, circus riding elephant in the room. That was torture!   So, I decided to strike up a lil' conversation.

"Honey, can we talk? I mean it's been such a great few days and I just wanna thank you for thinking enough of us to get away from it all for a few. I think I really needed this and didn't realize how much I did."

"Anything you wanna say? I mean you know you can **ALWAYS** tell me anything and I do mean **ANYTHING**." Okay this has to be the moment of truth. I just know it's coming out now. I can see it on his brain trickling down to his tongue now. 1, 2, 3...go!

"Nothing babe. I'm glad you are enjoying yourself. I figured you needed it and I needed to get some chill time too."

Hey wait... you mean that's it?! That's all I get? Are you serious?! You mean I give you the opportunity to come clean and you don't?! What the Heaven?! Okay, ok, ok.... it's time to regroup. What's plan B, because I am gonna get the truth out of him if it kills him or if I do first. I know, let me get him in the mood and that will get him talking. No.... wait, if I do that he might think that something is wrong. But what the heck, it's worth a try.

"Hey baby... come in here. I got a nice surprise for you. I mean you went through all this trouble to get me up here and the least I could do is to thank you appropriately."

Oh huh, did you say something babe? I couldn't hear you. (Comes in dressed and ready to go out). I'll be back in a few babe. Gonna go get something to cook to eat before we go. (Kisses me on the cheek as he walks out the door).

Oh, never mind. "Oh, I just said that I really needed this time away."

(Sigh) Ok, ok, ok. I will not call him. I will not call him. I will **NOT** call him. Ugh... why did he leave me here by myself. Ok, no, I have got the willpower to do this. (Staring at the phone)

Let me find something to do. That's great to say in a place where there is ABSOLUTELY NOTHING to do!!!! I am determined not to call him but this darn phone is staring at me and following me everywhere I go. Oh.... what the heck?!

I mean it's just a phone conversation and it's not like Rob and I are more than just

64

friends... or are we? Ughhhhh!!!!!!!!!!! I'm not going to get any rest with this on my mind sooooo here goes.

(Dialing the number) Ooooh...it's ringing... and ringing... and ringing... and ringing. Thank you God that he is not picking up... this **must** be a sign.

Face Value: Is What You See What You Get?

Chapter 12

Far Fetched

"Hello"

"Hello"?

Are you serious?! But what happened to the sign that you just gave me Lord?! I refused to say something and the NOT breathing was about to cause me to pass out. Oh Lord, he answered the phone. I thought you were on MY side (looking towards heaven). Dang! What now?

"I know it's you." he said.

Hammit!! Ok, ok, ok, ok.... what do I do?

"Uh, hey there, I was just about to hang up. It rang so long that I thought you weren't there."

"I'm sorry, I was downstairs and didn't really hear the phone. What's up? It's really great to hear from you."

Great to hear from me?! Does that mean he was thinking about me? If I didn't think I'd break something, I'd be doing cartwheels right about now. But wait.... noooooooooooo!

This is not the person I am supposed to be doing cartwheels over. It's supposed to be my HUSBAND that I get this excited for, not some random guy I met online. But the truth of the matter is that my husband is not here and right about now, I really need to hear some sweet soothing words that make me whooooo chile!

Yeah, I was thinking about you too. How have you been? What's new?

"I've got this newness that I've been finishing up."

Oh no! DON'T SAY IT!

"Wish you could come through and take a listen."

Ugh......he said it!

"So, can you?"

Can I what? (As if I didn't know what he was asking. Well at least it bought me some more time.)

"Uh, yeah sure, I can come by. What time?"

What time?! What was I thinking and how am I going to pull this off...again? Ok, what was I going to say as my excuse this time? I know it's gotta be something wrong with me asking God to help me out again with an excuse, but I guess I'm just not ready to learn *whatever* lesson all of this is supposed to tech me. The ironic thing or I guess I should say the hypocritical thing is the fact that I am the one called to help other people get out and stay out of these type situations.

68

But do I *really* have a *situation?* I mean it's not like we have been physically intimate or anything. We are just basically talking and sharing our ideas and thoughts about our ideas. Right.... or am I really in denial as to what is actually happening? Dang it! I can't believe this is happening to me. How did I let things get this far? You know what's even sadder is the fact that I really don't feel any regrets. I mean isn't the whole point of life about being honest with yourself and knowing where you are and being honest with God?

I know that you are reading this and thinking "Is she really serious right now?" Yes, I am really serious right now. The pastor, wife, author, motivational speaker, leader or women, counselor is serious about how I feel. Maybe that's the problem, since I have been called into this thing, NOBODY ever thinks to ask me how I feel. I just want to be normal! Is there a such thing as normal anymore? Ok, I got that out, now back to my reality.

I just really feel like there is a reason all of this is happening to me. But what is it?

(The front door opens)

"Hey love. What's all that?"

"I told you that this was going to be your weekend. So, I just went out and got a few things so that we won't have to leave and we can stay here the entire weekend undisturbed. Now, give me your phone and laptop because there will be no need for either. As a matter of fact, I'm going to put them in the safe."

Safe?! Is this really happening? Is he crazy? It was NOT supposed to go down like this!

"Uh babe, what if the church needs to reach me? I mean I kinda need to be able to be reached."

"I have already taken care of all of that. They know to contact Pastor Derris or Deacon Brown."

Since when did he become so concerned? And he did what?! You know he really does have some nerve pretending that he really wants to be up here with me. When I know all the time that the only reason I am here is because ole girl couldn't make it. Which by the way, reminds me of the real reason why I should not feel the least bit guilty in making plans to "visit" Rod. Why is it that he gets to pretend like nothing is happening and I have to be the moral righteous majority? I think I just might go ahead and get this all out in the open.

"You know..."

"Uh, babe wait, there is something I have got to tell you."

Yeah, like the combination to that safe!

"There is another reason that I brought you here this weekend. Well, the truth is that I need to come clean about some things. Uh, I haven't been the person that I need to be to you. I know that you have had a lot lately on your plate and if it seems like I have been distant and tired, it's because I have been. The truth of the matter is that I've been feeling a little neglected and found myself spending time with someone else."

There I was with a blank stare on my face. Is he really telling me this? Is he really telling me this in the middle of nowhere and expecting me to be okay with this? And what does he expect me to say... do?

"With all the time you have been spending at the church, I found myself just having conversation that started on the internet and unfortunately, it just kinda turned into more than just conversation. But trust me, it was only once. But I ended it because God convicted me and I really want to be your husband. Baby, I love you."

"What? You love me and you're sorry and it only happened once. So, tell me this DJ, why is it that she texted you to say that her plans changed and that she could still come up if you wanted her to? Yeah, that's right, I saw the text as you went on to say, and I quote 'I've decided to take my wife instead.' So you want to blame my being at the church for your being a jackass....really? How dumb do you think I am? What, the good right Reverend is supposed to just say a prayer and forgive you and we move on from what you just told me because you just decided to repent 'cause you really want to be with me or because your tail just got caught?!"

"But babe, you have got to believe me when I say it's over and that I really want this to work. I know you saw the text. I didn't know how to tell you so I purposely left my phone out hoping that you would see it and it would soften the blow a little."

What was I doing? I mean was I not being a noble hypocrite? Well, I guess not really, because he *actually* took it beyond the talking, meeting and thinking... he actually did 'it'!

"I, I, I, I just need some time.... I need some fresh air."

Hey, I did it! I just realized that I got my 'get out of jail free' card. So, should I call this, oh I don't know.... favor? Wait, did I just really say favor?! Yeah, I know.... delusional is the right word. So here I go with this freedom card with the right to do whatever I want to do. There's only one problem, my phone was still in that damn safe! (Sigh) Ok, let me think. It's 20 degrees out here and I have not a clue where the heck I am but, it won't hurt to try. Besides, I *really* want him to feel this thing and how he hurt me. So here I go to find my way to some kind of civilization.

So, I just happen to get in the car and just down the road I find a gas station and general store I guess, you'd say. The only thing on my mind is 'him'. I'm praying that he is going to pick up the phone and say just what I need him to say. What is it that I need him to say? You know, I really don't know. Maybe it's just the sound of his voice. Sometimes I realize that he can say so much without even saying so much. I just feel the kindness and care and love and concern in his voice. This is clearly something that I miss from DJ and I honestly, don't know how to get it back. Am I really pulling up into this place to call another man to help me with the woes of the one who is supposed to help me? Looks like I really am.

"Good evening, ma'am"

"Hi there, is there a phone I can use."

"Why sure. Just feel free to dial 9 and then it will allow you to get to who you need to get to. (smiling)"

"Great. Thank you!" (shivering)

Am I really dialing 'him'? This is what I need right now. God please let him be there. (phone ringing)

"Hello"

"Hey, there, it's me. H-h-how are you?"

"Hey, love, what's goin' on? I thought you forgot about me. What's going on? Are you okay? I mean I didn't hear back from you so I really didn't know what to think."

"(Sigh) I'm okay, uh I'm sorry for not contacting you sooner. I didn't forget about our date. I mean no not date but us getting together."

(He laughs.... oooo that voice!) "Feel free to call it what you want. So, where are you? Where do you want me to meet you?"

Ugh, ok, I mean it's just me getting together with a friend and sharing my thoughts and feelings with someone who understands me completely. Well at least that's my part of the

Face Value: Is What You See What You Get?

story and I'm sticking to it. Don't even talk to me about consequences right now because I'm not even trying to hear it. God, I need this right now in order for me to go on and if I'm going to be true to myself. Besides, where is my restitution in this matter?!

I gotta go or else I will be forever wonder what this could be and if I am missing out on the one person I get to understand me. Nobody knows what it's like to have to understand everyone and no one seems to even want to understand you not even your own husband.

"Hello? Are you ok? I mean if this is not a good time, we can reschedule."

"Oh, hey, no, no...I'm ok. Uh just let me know where to meet you and I'm there."

"Ok, how about our usual?"

"Actually, there is a place that is about an hour and a half outside of town that I really love to visit. Do you mind meeting me there?

"Ok, sounds good...see you in about an hour and a half."

What is it about him that makes me so nervous? I do remember that feeling when DJ and I first got together, however, unfortunately that excitement wore off rather quickly as life became real. It wore off even more when reality hit as I was truly honest about why I married him.

What is really going on here?! I feel like I am this whole other person that I don't even recognize anymore.

Normally the ride to this spot would have been kinda' boring but because I knew he would be there, it was quite soothing this time. I park the car and as I enter the spot, I am met with the sound of applause, snaps and rhymes.

My eyes go directly to him. There he is. Oh, my Lord why does he have to look so good?! Okay honey, get it together.

"Hey."

"Hey there love. You look rather nice this evening." (He stands to give me a much needed hug.)

I had to pry myself loose although I really didn't want to. It's just always such a breath of fresh air when I'm around him.

"So, how have you been? Are you sure you're okay? You look a little bothered."

"I, I'm fine just some things at home."

"So, how's that working out for you? Oh, man I'm sorry, that was way out of line."

"No, no, it's okay you're fine. Thanks for asking. I actually found out that he was having an affair. Um, yeah."

"Awwww wow, I'm so sorry. Are you okay?"

"Yeah, I'm fine. No. I'm not fine. I really don't know what to think or do or say."

"I bet I know what will make you feel better." (Smiling)

Okay, tell me he isn't talking about whisking me away to his place and ministering to my mind, body and soul. Apparently, my mind was already there.

"Chanda? Hello.... Chanda?" (Waving his hand in front of me)

"Huh? Ohhhh, I'm so sorry. I don't know where my mind was (well, actually yeah I do)."

Chapter 13

Coming to the Stage

"I was saying I think I know exactly what you need." He nods toward the stage while looking right into my eyes.

"Oh, oh no, I'm not ready. At least not for that stage."

"Uh, you are forgetting that I know what you can do."

Wow! This man is prompting and pushing for me to share my work at a time like this? Should I really try this?

"Come on, I'll be right here cheering you on and besides I already turned your name in."

"But I don't have anything prepared."

"Yeah, right. You are forgetting that I know where your thoughts lie and the prepared pen and paper isn't always it with you. You always have something prepared in your heart."

I couldn't believe that I was really getting up out of the chair to go up on a stage in front of all of these people and share my life, my words, my thoughts....my very being. Well, here goes.

The announcer: "Next gracing the stage tonight is an infant to us. She comes to us from the A. Let's give it up for C-Quel"

Thunderous applause filled the atmosphere.

C-Quel? Where in the heck did that come from? So, I quickly turn to look at Rod and all I see is this huge grin and then a wink that almost totally threw me off.

"Uh, hello, everybody. Um, I'm Chan....C-Quel and tonight I want to give you just a peek into my world. I call this one......

The Call

The more I listen the better I hear,
I hear the sound of Jesus standing near.
I haven't always chosen to listen to His call,
Then I realize that without it is how I fall.
I fall into things and don't know how I got there,
Sometimes I feel like I'm in a race like the Tortoise and the Hare.
There are times when I just wanna quit because I'm tired,
But then I get this nudge to get back on track and on the job 'cause ain't nothing like gettin' fired.
I'm not afraid to admit that sometimes I fall short,
God please don't leave me because your daughter needs you to touch her heart.

78

Touch me and hold me and draw me closer to you,

For this season I'm in, only You can bring me through.

"Thank you for listenin'."

The announcer: "Ladies and gentlemen, whoooooo, let's give it up for C-Quel. Girl did her thing didn't she?!"

"Thank you for having me."

When I left the stage, I looked around and not only did I hear the applause and snaps but folks were standing up and yelling. Really? I mean all of this for me an infant to this type of stage? I can't even lie, it was like a feeling I never felt before. I was in a place of euphoria.

As I made my way back to the table where Rod was sitting, I couldn't help but think about how he believed in me enough to push me because he saw beyond me and saw ME. I know I should be thankful and I am but now this complicates things even more. Dang!

"Awwww, watch out now....look at you! I thought you said you had never done this before. I mean if that's true, I sure couldn't tell."

He gives me a high five and then hugs me tightly.

"Ahhhh, that was exhilarating! How can I ever thank you?"

"Just seeing you up there was thanks enough."

I glanced down at my watch and realized that it was after midnight. "Oh, wow, I didn't realize it was this late. Uh, I really need to get back."

"Ok, hey, let me walk you out."

"Oh, no, I'm okay really...."

He looks at me with this 'let me do this' look.

"My car is this way." As we are walking next to each other, I am hoping and wondering if he can hear my heart pounding at least 1000 beats per minute.

"Look, I want to really thank you again for pushing me to get up there tonight. I mean, it was just what I needed to take my mind off of things."

"It was my pleasure and I knew that you could do it. Um listen, I'm sorry about you and your husband and if you need to talk, you know I'm here."

"Thank you and thank you for walking me to my car. So, I guess I will talk to you later."

There was a brief silence and then he reached out to hug me and as I reluctantly return the hug (ha!), I heard......

"You know you really don't have to go back."

"No. I think I'd better, I mean I don't know where we are in this thing yet and I don't want to make any rash or hasty decisions."

"I meant tonight. You don't have to go back tonight. It is rather late and I'm not really keen on you having to drive that far in the dark. You did say it took you about an hour to get here right?"

"Yeah, ummmm, I appreciate the offer and I really think that I will be okay."

"Check your phone."

I go to grab my phone and realize that it's still in the safe at the cabin.

"Uh, I don't have my phone with me. It's a long story."

"So, he let you leave without your phone?"

"Actually, he doesn't even know I'm gone. I mean he knows I'm gone but just not how far or that I'm here."

"So, he knew that you left and let you leave without your phone. I'm just saying, please stay here just until the morning so you can see clearly....the road I mean."

Oh honey, this takes things to a whoooooole other level! Spend the night?! With him?! I can't even believe that I am actually considering it. But he does have a point. I mean DJ knew I was leaving and let me leave without my phone. (Sigh) I promise myself that I will let nothing happen.

"Look, I promise that as soon as light hits, I will make sure you are up and on your way. I just want you to be safe."

"Okay, you talked me into it and I am kinda tired. Being deep really wears you out."

"I'm parked just up the street and you can follow me."

So I get in my car and still shocked at the fact that I am following another man home. But hey, at least he really cares about my well-being. Again, the ride was a soothing one but also a somewhat convicting one. I mean, what was I doing?!

"So, here we are. You can park in my spot."

Wow! I mean I thought I was imagining things. This place is immaculate! The loft I have been dreaming of forever. Okay, calm down and don't lose sight of why you are here honey. We proceed to walk upstairs and as my foot hit every step, it was like my eyes were open to a new world.

"Uh, make yourself comfortable and you can have my bed tonight."

He must have seen my eyes get extremely big and heard my heart stop completely.

"I mean my bed without me in it of course. I will be right here on the couch. If you need something to change into, feel free to grab a t-shirt if you'd like."

"Hey, Rod, I really want to thank you for everything. It's been a while since I have been made to feel special."

"Hey, I understand and I'd want someone to do the same for the women in my life. I mean have a mother, sister, nieces, and would want a guy to do the same for them. Hey once you get settled, would you like some coffee?"

"Sure, that would be great......thanks!" So, I make my way to his room and actually put on one of his t-shirts over my pants that smell oh

so good. I walk into the living room and take a seat on the couch.

"Hey, I see you found something and not too bad I might add. Here's your coffee." He takes a seat on the opposite end of the couch."

Jesus help me!

Face Value: Is What You See What You Get?

Chapter 14

The Dawn of a New Day

By the time I actually went to bed, it was about 3:30am. I can't tell you how refreshing it was to talk about absolutely everything I felt and not feel like I was just babbling or someone was listening because they were 'supposed' to be. I mean he actually listened and responded with clarity and interest. To be totally honest, I wasn't even sure if I wanted to go back just yet. He was such a gentleman. I couldn't help but remember when DJ was like this and how it was this that won me over. It was him treating me like I was the only woman in the world.

Knock, knock, knock...."Chanda, are you awake?"

As I slowly rub my eyes to help me wake up, for a moment I got confused at the sound of this voice. I looked around the room and soon realized that it was *not* a dream and that I really was here. I am in another man's place. I jumped to my feet and told him to *come in.*

"Hey, how did you sleep? Well, let me put it this way, from what I heard, you slept pretty well. I know it's kind of late but I really didn't want to wake you."

"Oh, wow... how embarrassing. I must apologize. It only happens when I'm really tired and besides you did have me up until almost the crack of dawn. I mean really, so technically, it is your fault."

"I took the liberty of whipping up a little breakfast, well now brunch to make sure you didn't have to stop and because you have been such a great and welcomed guest."

"Awe, you really didn't have to so that. I mean you have already done enough. But, a sista is kinda hungry. I'll be right out."

As I am getting dressed, I can't help but begin to think about DJ. I wonder what he might be thinking. I wonder if he even noticed that the car was gone and I was gone in it and if he's even tried to look for me. Sadly, even though I am here is this place that I have always dreamed of, I can't help but wish that it was DJ and not Rod here.

As I exited his bedroom, I walked upon one of the most beautiful sights I'd ever seen. The table was set with the most beautiful floral centerpiece with the most delectable looking dishes. You can tell this was not a fly by night job and that he did it with sincerity. All I could do was stand there for a moment and take it all in.

"Is everything okay? What, do you see something that you don't like?"

"Um....no, everything is just perfect. I mean more that I could imagine. This is unbelievable. Thank you."

"Here, have a seat."

He proceeds to pull a chair out for me.

We sat and talked for about another hour or so. "Oh, I really need to get going but thank you for everything. I really mean it."

I went to get my shoes and gathered my thoughts enough to push myself to leave. *"Well, I can't say tha...."*

"Chanda you don't have to keep saying thank you. It was my pleasure to do all of it. Really it was. I just wish we could do more of it. I mean the whole poetry thing of course. But under the circumstances, I understand if you can't or if I may not see or hear from you in a while."

We stand and stare in silence. I wonder what he's thinking.

"Hey, get outta here before I have to keep you again. Um, let me know when you get there."

"I will."

As I turned to walk out the door and feel a gentle touch on my hand. Oh no.... please no. Anything but this! I couldn't help but stop and slowly turn around. Before I knew it, his lips were passionately pressed against mine. I knew it was wrong but I didn't want him to stop. This was a moment I wanted, a moment I needed even if it wasn't from my husband. For once in a long time, I felt loved, I felt needed, I felt beautiful, noticed and well...I felt free.

As I came back to my senses, I pushed him away in shock more so that anything.

"Oh wow, I'm so sorry. I don't know where that came from. Please forgive me. I honestly meant no disrespect to you or your husband."

"Nothing happened that I didn't want to happen. I'll be in touch...soon."

I decided to take the scenic route back to the cabins so I could think through all of this. As I walked into the cabin's door. I hear the sound of snoring. It's 3 in the afternoon... really? I walk into the bedroom and purposely drop my things on the floor. He finally rose up and said, *"Oh hey babe, glad you made it back. Did you clear your head like you needed to?"*

You mean I have been gone for almost 24 hours and there was no gift, no candlelit meal, no search party... NOTHING! Now see, this is just the very thing that makes me **not** regret what I did.

"You want something to eat? I'm sorry if you tried to call. I was just exhausted."

"Um how could I call when you have my phone locked up in a safe? But thanks anyway for your concern. I need to take a shower. This is your trip so whatever you have planned is fine and yes, I did get a chance to clear my head." More that you will ever know.

"I'll have something ready when you get out of the shower. I thought we'd watch a movie and just chill tonight and maybe go into town in the morning and then head home."

"That's fine."

I was saying that's fine but all I could think about was Rod. Oh shoot, I need to let him know that I made it here. My phone is locked away but his isn't. If I could just grab it and put it back on the table without him ever noticing. I turned on the shower and let it run. I tip-toed into the room after hearing him turn on some music in the kitchen. I had to do it fast before he missed his phone (which I'm convinced is his second love. I'm not even sure if I know who or what his first love is anymore.)

I began to text then realized that I need to be able to erase any trace of the number. I decided to call instead because I really needed and wanted to hear his voice.

(The phone ringing) "Hey, just wanted to let you know that I made it back safe and sound. Thank you again aaaand I will definitely call you when I get back."

"Thanks for calling me and I look forward to hearing from you...soon."

I hurried and erased the number, put the phone back and jumped in the shower. No sooner than I hit the water, I heard him call... *"Babe, you okay? I thought I heard you say something."*

"Hey, no, I'm fine. I was just thinking out loud."

We sat and enjoyed our evening together as we watched all of *his* favorite movies or should I say as the movies watched him. Meanwhile, all I could do was think about where I was last night and the freedom I experienced. How could I get back there? Later that night we tried to make it memorable but to me it doesn't count if you fall asleep in the middle of 'snoreplay'.

We got up the next morning, packed our things and headed for home. To be honest, although it was Sunday morning, I didn't miss the hustle and bustle of the church. That was one good thing that he did that I am thankful for in taking care of things while I was away. I didn't realize how much I needed to get away. Although things were not quite how I imagined them to be, it was definitely an eye opener. I did make sure to get my phone before leaving. The ride home was unusually quiet as if he knew something was up.

Chapter 15

I Don't Even Know Anymore

No sooner than we got into the house, the phone started ringing. I almost hated to answer it but did anyway. Although, they knew I was on vacation, there were still things that needed to be done.

"Hey babe, um I need to run over to the church for about an hour. I promise I'll be back and we can finish our evening." Hey, don't judge me, I am trying to make this work.

Of course, when I got in the car, I grabbed my phone. I was about to call him and looked and saw that I had 3 text messages. I just assumed that they were from the church members or definitely from Diahmion. I stopped at the end of the driveway and saw that all 3 were from Rod.

'I want to apologize again for my actions; I really didn't want to disrespect you. I hope that we can still hang out at The Stage because you really have something great inside of you that needs to come out. If you still want.... please feel free to hit me up....RodLoft.'

'I got your messages and trust me there is nothing to apologize for. And yes, The Stage is still a go. TTYS.'

No sooner than I pressed 'send' my phone began to ring and of course this time it was my girl Diah.

"Yes, ma'am, how may I help you?"

"Hey lovely, welcome back! How was your trip? You know we missed you this weekend, especially this morning. But you will be proud to know that Rev. *Shoutawood brought it girl! We had 10 to come down for membership and salvation!*"

"Praise God! I must call him when I get settled."

"Um, wait, why are you on the phone anyway and y'all are still supposed to be on vacation?"

"Do you even need to ask? You know how that goes. Anyway, I'm on my way to the church."

"So, what are you doing tomorrow my dear? Let's do lunch if possible."

"You got it. Listen, let me run in here for a quick second and I just let me know when and where for tomorrow. Love you!"

"Okay love...see ya!"

I met up with Diahmion for lunch the next day and before I could say anything, she actually said something to me. *"Okay.... spill it."*

"What are you talking about?"

"I talked to a friend of mine and for some reason I feel there is something that you need to tell me."

"A friend of yours?" Oh, so now she wants to admit something.

"Okay, since you won't tell me then I will tell you. Or do the words The Stage mean anything to you?"

"How do you know about that?!"

"Rod told me. He didn't mention any names but I knew he was talking about you. Girl, what did you do to him?"

"I didn't do **anything** to him. I simply did a piece, it got late, I spent the night at his place, he made breakfast, we kissed before I left and I went back to the cabin with DJ. So, you see nothing happened."

"Are you crazy?! You call that nothing? Chanda, what is wrong with you.... what are you thinking? Do you realize that if this gets out that it could ruin things for you, your marriage and the church?"

"And how do you propose people will find out? Especially since you are not going to say anything and The Stage is at least 100 miles from here. You know what, I have had enough of this conversation for today. Thank you for lunch and for your concern, but I think I can handle my own affairs. Uh.... don't go there, you know what I mean."

For the next few days, I tried to occupy my mind with church work but all I could think about was The Stage and how it made me feel, how Rod made me feel, how DJ made me feel and the reality of what Diahmion said. I was really trying to stay focused. But was I really risking anything? I mean it was just me doing what I love to do. I wasn't hurting anybody.

Without even telling him, I had to prove that I was doing this for myself. I rode out to The Stage just to get away from it all. I thought I was incognito when all of a sudden, I heard.... *"Hey, C-Quel! What's up love? Please tell me you came to grace The Stage tonight."*

It was Slate the announcer.

"Hey there. Uh, no, I just came to listen tonight."

"Well, feel free to let me know if you change your mind."

I hung around for about an hour and a half and as I was getting up to leave, I heard, "Pastor?"

I know they couldn't be talking to me so I kept walking. "Pastor Chanda?"

Oh no.... what am I supposed to do? So, I turned around and lo and behold there was Adrian, one of the youth from the church that went off to college. "Adrian? Hey sweetie, how are you? What are you doing here?"

"Oh, some friends and I come here sometimes just to chill and get away. How are you? I really miss the church and hope to be home to visit real soon. What are you doing here, if you don't mind me asking?"

"Funny, I too come here to get away sometimes. And yes, we miss you too and look forward to having you home to visit. Listen, it was good to see you and you guys, take care. Hope all is well."

Oh, snap, this is just what I didn't want to happen. Thank you Diahmion for speaking this into existence. I am just praying that she won't tell her nosey mama that she saw me.

Oh well, back to the drawing board and back to work.

On the way back home, I couldn't help but to make a phone call. "Hey there, I'm in the neighborhood and just thought I'd give you a call."

"Hey there. I thought you went MIA on me. Well, I'm here if you want to stop by for a few."

"Okay, I'm actually right around the corner."

I parked my car and headed up to the loft. Before I could even knock on the door, I heard... *"It's open, come on in. I'm in the kitchen."*

No hugging, no touching Chanda!

"Hey, am I interrupting something? I can come back later."

"Would you get in here. (laughing) I heard you were at the spot."

"Dang, news travels fast."

"Yeah, my boy Slate hit me up I guess because he thought we'd be together. So, what made you go?"

"Your boy Slate? Ohhhh, so you let me think you had no idea about this place. You tricked me! I man, I don't know. I just really needed to get away and clear my head and that was the only place I felt I could do that and be free."

"Well I'm glad you did. Uh...how's everything going?"

"If I'm here then that should answer quite a lot. I mean it's 'complicated'."

"Look, you know I'm here if you need me. I mean as a friend and nothing else. Are you hungry?"

"I don't know. It depends on what you burnin' up in there."

"Awww see there you go with the jokes. You've tasted what I have before so you know what I can do."

"Excuse me?"

"See there you go now, get your mind out of the gutta girl. You know what I mean. Did you not leave here full the last time you were here?"

"Yeah, yeah, yeah. I must admit you put it on me real good."

"Uh, excuse me?"

"Now see there you go. Get your mind out the gutta guy."

We both begin to laugh and before you know it, weeks went by and my schedule got extremely hectic but I managed to get it all done without anything lacking. I can't lie, Rod really made things a whole lot easier to handle. Things with DJ and I were still the same and Diahmion was still sending out her smoke signals to warn me of the potential dangers and error of my ways. But, I kept preaching, church was awesome as we were getting more members now than we had in a long time. For some reason I had more energy than I had in a long time and yes, I must thank Rod for showing me the fountain of youth.

Things were seemingly going well when the unthinkable happened.

Rod and I went to The Stage one night and I was coerced into doing a piece. As I got up on the stage and got into my piece, I looked out into the crowd and there was DJ. Yes, DJ standing in the back and looking directly at me. Needless to say, all I could do was freeze. Right in the middle of my piece I froze but I knew I had to finish or else that would damage me as an artist. Thank God the audience thought it was a part of the piece. As usual, the applause and snaps were thunderous. What was I going to do about getting off of this stage? I asked Slate for a glass of water and exited stage left. I needed a moment to think. I walked out the back door and ran to my car. I told Slate to tell Rod I had to leave because I wasn't feeling well.... God knows I was not lying this time.

I was afraid to pull up in the driveway but knew I had to face the music. As soon as I opened the door....

"How long, Chanda?!"

I froze again and didn't answer. I knew what was possibly about to happen and I felt like time had stopped.

"I asked you a question, "How long?!"

"What are you talking about and why are you shouting?"

"Don't play with me. I saw you tonight. Who is he and how long?"

"He's just a friend who has been helping me with my poetry.... that's all."

"You still didn't answer my question. Who is he and how long has he been 'helping' you?"

"Are you drunk? Look, I'm tired and you need to relax. We'll talk about this in the morning."

"No. We will talk about it now!"

Before I knew it, I was grabbing my face and getting up from off of the floor. Wait....is this for real?

"Are you crazy?! What is wrong with you?! Don't you ever put your hands on me again in your life!"

"Chanda! Chanda! Chanda, don't you dare walk out of here when I'm trying to talk to you."

"Talk?! Talk?! Look at my face. Does that look like talking to you?! Don't bother looking for me again, as if you would anyway. I'm out!"

(Knocking on the door)

"Who is it?"

"Rod, it's me."

"Chanda? What are you doing here? What happened to your...did he hit you?!"

"Rod, I can't do it anymore. I can't.... please just hold me."

"Hey sure baby, come on in. Let me clean you up and you can stay here tonight."

"I, I........."

"Shhhhh.... you don't have to say anything. Just let me get you settled. We can talk tomorrow."

The next thing I knew, I was lying next to Rod as he cradled me in his arms and rubbed my head until I must have fallen asleep. Somehow, I woke up in the middle of the night and I guess I jumped because I was oblivious as to where I was.

"Hey, hey, hey...I'm here, I'm here, I'm here. Are you okay? What happened?"

"DJ saw us last night at The Stage and confronted me when I got home but I realized he was drunk and I refused to talk to him. That's when he hit me. He's never done that before. It was like he was in a rage. That's when I left and came here."

"Do you need me to handle him for you?"

"No, I don't want to cause any further damage. I just appreciate you being here for me."

My lips were immediately drawn to his as he caressed my face and looked deep into my eyes. As my hands felt every muscle on his back, I felt the earth move like never before. I didn't want it to ever end. Little did he know, he had cradled my mind and my soul and spirit long before this moment. This was just the tip of the iceberg as he had already become familiar with the depths of me. I knew it was wrong and I had possibly reached the point of no return but after all I had been through, I didn't even care.

At daybreak, I saw his repeat performance as he made breakfast again as this time was even more-lovely than the first. I knew I had to eventually face reality and wrap my head around what was really goin' on. I turned on my phone and saw 15 missed calls. Some from DJ and the others from Diahmion. The next thing I heard was Rod saying that I was at his place and that I was a little shaken up but I was okay.

"I'll be sure to tell her to call you."

As I walk into the room... "Let me guess, Diahmion right?"

"Uh, yeah, she was just calling because she said your husband called her upset and frantic because he didn't know where you had gone. How are you feeling? Let me take a look at your face. Damn, baby, that's going to take some time to heal. Are you sure you don't want me to talk to him?"

"Yes, I'm sure. Thanks again for letting me."

"What did I tell you before about that whole thank you thing? Seriously, I meant it when I told you that I am here for you. Chanda...I love you."

Wait! Did he just say what I think he said? Did he just say he loved me? Oh, that's just great. Why not complicate things even more than they already are?! (Sigh) So I mean what am I supposed to say to that? Do I love him and if I do can I say it when I am married to someone else who I am only supposed to say it to? Dear God...help me please!

Suddenly his phone rings and he states that he has to go in to work for a few hours and I am more than welcomed to stay at the loft. Whew! Thank you for divine intervention although I know eventually it's going to come up again. *"Thanks, but I'm going to try to go home and if I need to, I'll be sure to call you for backup."*

I go and get dressed and take a long look at my face. He really did a number on me.

As I'm driving, I'm praying and thinking about what to say. Now I know you are saying she has some nerve praying when I got myself into all of this. But, yes, I am praying. I pull up in the driveway and think to myself 'let's try this again'.

I open the door and DJ is sitting at the kitchen table with his face in his hands. When I close the door, he looks up and moves toward me. I jump and immediately tense up.

"Baby, I...I.... I...I'm sooo sorry. I really don't know what happened or what got into me. You know that I have NEVER, EVER hit you before."

All I could do was sit down and give a blank stare. I mean, what was I supposed to say....do? *"I just need some space."*

So, I got up and walked out of the room hoping he wouldn't follow me because I REALLY didn't know what to say. As I made my way upstairs, I heard silence and then all of a sudden, it was a sound that I had NEVER heard before. DJ was actually crying!

Should I go and see what was wrong with him or is it a trick? (SIGH)

As I sat in the room, with the door ajar just enough to hear him sobbing, so many things went through my mind. Despite everything that was going on, I had to admit that I truly do love my husband but then what do I do with these feelings about Rod? Was that just a façade or my plea for attention?

I couldn't bring myself to go back down there. Hours passed in complete silence. Then I heard the car keys and the door slam. I was a bit hesitant but I got up and proceeded to look out the bedroom window and I saw him get in the car. For a brief moment I wanted to run and call him back. I stood in the window and we locked eyes for a few seconds like we hadn't in a long time. I knew from that look that something was still there. He backed out of the driveway and drove down the street.

No sooner than he left, my phone went off. God, please not now. It was Deacon Brown. "Hey there Deac. What's going on?"

"Uh hey there Pastor, uh we were wondering if everything was okay?"

"Yeah, everything is fine.... why?"

"Well, the board is here waiting on you for the emergency meeting."

Ugghhhh... I can't believe that I did it again! This is becoming a really bad habit. I have got to get a handle on things.

"Tell everybody to stay right there. I am on my way."

"Okkkk, I'll try. Take your time and be careful."

I got ready as fast as I could considering I had to cover my face as best I could and tried to drive like I had some sense. To my surprise I pulled up and the members of the board were still there. I jumped out of the car (out of breath no doubt) and literally ran in the building. Amidst the stares and bewildered looks, the meeting went on without a hitch. I decided to stay awhile and do some things in my office.

"Good night Pastor.... don't stay here too long by yourself. We'll set the alarm when we leave. Now are you sure you will be okay?"

"Yea, yea, I will be just fine. I promise I won't be long...promise. (My head tilted with a smile)"

As I say goodnight to the board, I walk down the hall to my office and hear a noise. Okay, yeah, that's not good when you are in a huge church by yourself. But, I kept walking and something pulled me toward the sanctuary. So reluctantly and with my cell phone in hand, I head that way. I'm thinking that it's Deacon Brown forgetting something.

"Deacon is that you? I thought I told you guys to go home and not to worry about me. Hey Deac...."

As I continue into the sanctuary, nobody says anything but I see this silhouette of a person at the altar.

Now REALLY hesitant and with my phone ready to press 911, I cautiously inch closer. "Hello, can I help you? Uh, the church is closed but you are more than welcome to some back tomorrow. Helloooo?"

The closer I get, I realize that the person is not a stranger.... it's.....

"DJ, is that you?" I walk even closer and yes not only is it him but I notice something in his hand. It was a gun! His hand was tightly wrapped around it as I stood completely frozen. *"DJ, what are you doing?! Where did you get a gun?!"*

"Chanda, I can't do this anymore. I don't know what happened to us. I can't do this!" (yelling)

"Do what?!" (still standing frozen)

"This, this game, this, this not knowing what is going on and having to pretend that we are okay." He sobs silently.... sitting still and grabs his head.

I feel the urge to slowly walk towards him. As I begin to walk, my phone rings. As it rings, I stop just long enough to look at it.

"I know it's him. Go ahead and answer it. You know you want to."

"It's not...."

"I said answer it!" (picking up the gun and standing up in my direction)

My heart pounding uncontrollably. I answer the phone with my hands shaking. *"Hello."*

"Hey you, I haven't heard from you and was just checking on you."

"Hey, I'm okay. How are you?"

"Are you sure you are okay?"

Grabbing the phone out of my hand, DJ puts the phone up to his ear and begins to speak. Has he really lost his mind?!

"She told you that she's fine."

"Hello? Um, hey man, I don't want any trouble so just put Chanda back on the phone. I'm just checking on her."

"Checking on her?! Why the do you feel the need to check on MY WIFE?!"

"Look man after what you did to her face, it's obvious that you have forgotten how to do your job."

"You know nothing about me or us! I love her!"

"Then why don't you start showing it because if you did, she wouldn't feel the need to come to me!"

"Rod, I'm okay." DJ turns and looks at me with fire in his eyes. This is a look that I have NEVER seen before.

"SHUT UP! You don't owe him nothing. I'm your husband Chanda....me not him! Why? Why do you feel the need to go to him?!"

"You really want to know?!" Just as I let those words come out of my mouth, I felt something behind me. I slowly turned around and it was Rob standing there and I just knew my life was over.

"Rob? How...how did you know where I was and how did you get in here?" No sooner had I asked those two questions than Diahmion walked in behind him. She said she saw DJ's car at the church and when she didn't get an answer at the house, she decided to grab Rob and stop by knowing that something had to be wrong.

"Look, y'all need to leave, this is between Chanda and me. Man, you especially need to get outta here, cause the way I feel right now, I could just blow you away!"

"Yo, man I ain't goin' nowhere until I know she safe. So if you gotta take me out then so be it."

Are you serious? This man is willing to take a bullet for me?! This is something that I NEVER EVER could imagine in my wildest dreams. Am I imagining this thing?!

"Wait! Everybody just calm down. DJ, put the gun down baby please. Let's talk about this."

Diahmion tries to use her phone to call the police.

"Diahmion, I love you but if you even think about calling the police, I'm not afraid to take you out either."

Was I really hearing this right?! Now I know he has lost his mind. He and Diahmion are like brother and sister.

Little did we all know, she was recording the entire thing.

"D, girl please just put the phone down....I don't think he's playin'."

Just as I was turning away from Diahmion, a very errie feeling came over me. I turned around and my nightmare got worse. I turned and DJ had the gun pointed directly between my eyes. Before Rob could say anything, he warned him not to try to be a hero.

"DJ, please, this is not what you want to do. Please, don't do this. We can work it out.... please!"

"Oh, so now you want to work it out? Where was all of this when you were with him.... huh?!"

"I tried to talk to you but you wouldn't listen! So, what was I supposed to do?! And don't even think that you are so innocent is all of this. Yeah, I saw the text messages from 'her'."

"She didn't mean anything to me. You left me and shut me out so YOU tell me what I was supposed to do?! I tried talking to you and all you could talk about was this damn church or how you and Diahmion were hanging out or how you wanted to light up the stage. So you tell me......where did I fit in.... huh....where?! Now you got this fool thinkin' that I don't care about my wife! Chanda since the first day I saw you, I loved you more than myself. You left me a long time ago. But I swear if I can't have you then I'll be damned if I let anyone else have you!"

My heart still pounding all the more now than ever. "Please, please, please DJ, I'm begging you not to do this. I'm sorry, I'm sorry. You killing me is not going to do anything to solve this. I'm sorry for turning my back on you.... baby, I didn't realize what was happening and I thought you didn't care. You never seem to want to know what I was doing or even acted as if you were concerned. That's why I threw myself into the church and D and Rob became my salvation. He listened to me."

"Look man, don't do this."

"I thought I told you to shut up! You're the reason we're here."

"No, YOU are the reason we're here! This woman loves you man and you are too blind to see it. Then again, maybe you are right. Maybe I am the reason that we are here. Maybe this is just what you need to get your attention. So, brother either you wake up or she's coming with me."

"Baby, please.... I'm sorry. You gotta believe me."

As I was talking, his hand began to tremble with the gun still in his hand pointing at my face. All I could do was stare him straight in his eyes. As I stared, there was something that took me back to when we first met. For the first time in a long time, I saw the man I loved."

As his hand trembled, he suddenly fell to his knees between my legs and cried. All I could do was drop and console him. But what do I do about Rob?

What do I do about my feelings for him or were my feelings even real? Rob quickly grabbed the gun and all I could do was look at him but with no words. When I looked up again, he and D were gone.

The next morning, I felt the need to call Rob and thank him. As I went to pick up the phone, something came over me and I couldn't even bring myself to dial. In addition, to that, DJ had just walked into the room and I did not want a repeat performance. When I went to log on to my computer, there was already a message that simply said... *"You're welcome."*

Face Value: Is What You See What You Get?

Chapter 16

Full Circle

I decided to take some time before the morning service to just share what I've been thinking. I needed to take a seat anyway because of the way I'd been feeling as of late. I really think that all of the events that have taken place have taken somewhat of a toll on my mind and seemingly my body. Anyway, I proceeded to write "Things have been very interesting for the past few days and I had to bring myself to the face the truth of what led to the week's scary events. The sermon may be a little different in that I have to ask for forgiveness of my husband before the entire congregation. Is it any of their business? No and I won't go into details but do feel like I needed to lead by example."

As I get up to walk down to the sanctuary, I feel a little dizzy and I'm not really sure why. The sermonic moment extremely well, thanks be to God! In that same service prior to the benediction, I expressed to the congregation that I was taking a hiatus and that the church would be in more than capable hands. The surprise was that DJ stood up and spoke which was kind of scary because I had *no* clue as to what he was going to say. The other surprise was that Rob showed up Sunday morning. Oh, yeah, you know a sister was still a little nervous.

After the benediction, I was greeting the congregants and still watching out of the corner of my eye to make sure part 2 wasn't about to go down. Low and behold to my chagrin, they were standing in front of each other shaking hands. What the heck?! Was I seeing things? Honey, only God could do a thing like this. As Rob approached me, we both knew that in some strange way, the romance that I thought was meant to be was actually sent to be my saving grace.

After this very strange encounter, I decided to go back to my office and finish jotting down some of my thoughts because this was not something that I wanted to forget. As soon as I got back to my office, again I had to immediately sit down. What the heck was going on with me today?! Maybe I'm just tired and really need a break.

Anyway, I sat down, got a sip of water and began to write.... "It's amazing how things change. As I thought about all of the events that took place, all I could think about was how we shout 'Amen' and not even know what we are agreeing to. It was time for me to pay closer attention myself to what I was agreeing to. I was called to my marriage first. Unfortunately, I was about to lose all of what we had worked so hard to gain. The church became my first love replacing my husband and my family. My friends became my console and I almost lost it all pursuing something that has its place that I have been graced to do. It wasn't that I couldn't live the life I wanted, but I wasn't supposed to do it alone.

It was great to scream and shout "Amen" on Sunday but what better place to holla than in my own home.... *"Praise the Lord everybody!"* "Let the church say Amen... again!" and really mean it this time."

I wanted to continue but had to stop because I really felt sick. I decided to ask DJ if he could bring me something to eat just to help settle my stomach. No sooner than he brought me something and I took a bite, I had to run immediately to the bathroom. I decided to take a nap on the couch in my office hoping that I'd feel better enough to get up and go home.

Almost an hour had passed and I decided that I'd go ahead and go home. I got home took a shower and went to bed.

The next morning, I woke up and just could not muster up enough energy to get out of bed. I didn't have a choice because there was so much I had to do today.

"Okay honey, you have got to get up and get yourself together." No sooner than I said these words, I had to literally run to the bathroom and up came everything that was in me. What the heck was really going on?

Ok, I can't continue like this. So, I called to make an appointment with the doctor. Thank God they have an opening and I can go now.

Huh? How could this happen? All I could think about were the words she kept saying to me... "Congratulations!" Me pregnant? Now? I don't know how DJ is going to feel about this. Wait. DJ and I haven't been....and she said that I'm already 8 weeks. No! God, please don't tell me this. Not now when we are just getting back on track. Could it be that the baby isn't his? I mean the only other explanation is that it's.... Oh my God!

About the Author

"But seek ye first the kingdom of God and his righteousness; and all these things shall be added unto you."-Matthew 6:33

Legena S. Crawford, a native of Savannah, Georgia, and is a product of the Atlanta Public Schools System. Upon graduating high school, she entered West Georgia College (presently the State University of West Georgia) where she received her undergraduate and graduate degrees in Early Childhood Education. It was there in 1993 she was honored to become a member of Delta Sigma Theta Sorority, Inc. As a profession, Legena is an elementary school teacher with over 20 years of experience in the Atlanta Public Schools System.

In 2003, along with her business partner founded and operated GenShon and Associates Consulting Firm, LLC specializing in Educational and Ministry Management consultation. She is currently the founder and lead consultant of The P.O.W.E.R Experience,

LLC, an organizational consulting firm specializing in contractual, ministry, individual and small business consulting.

She has served in ministry for over 25 years. She has served on numerous ministries as a leader and servant. She currently serves as the Executive/Co-Pastor of Strong Tower Christian Life Ministries in Stone Mountain, Georgia.

Legena is blessed to be happily married to Robert W. Crawford of Augusta, Georgia and the mother of one son. She enjoys writing, acting, singing, and spending time with her family and friends. Daily she strives to make herself available to God's will and God's way. Her life's thought is "Your life is a gift from God and what you do with it is your gift to Him."

www.ingramcontent.com/pod-product-compliance
Lightning Source LLC
Chambersburg PA
CBHW072233290326
41934CB00008BA/1282